EVERY
POSSESSION
HAS A HISTORY

Rebecca Vickers

Raintree is an imprint of Capstone Global Library Limited, a company incorporated in England and Wales having its registered office at 7 Pilgrim Street, London, EC4V 6LB Registered company number: 6695582

www.raintreepublishers.co.uk
myorders@raintreepublishers.co.uk

Text © Capstone Global Library Limited 2014
First published in hardback in 2014
The moral rights of the proprietor have been asserted.

Edited by Andrew Farrow, James Benefield, and Adrian Vigliano
Designed by Tim Bond
Original illustrations © Capstone Global Library Ltd 2014
Picture research by Liz Alexander
Originated by Capstone Global Library Ltd
Production by Victoria Fitzgerald

Printed and bound in China

ISBN 978 1 406 27277 2
17 16 15 14 13
10 9 8 7 6 5 4 3 2 1

British Library in Cataloguing Data
A full catalogue record for this book is available from the British Library.

Acknowledgements

We would like to thank the following for permission to reproduce photographs: Alamy pp. 8 (© Pictorial Press Ltd), 22 (© CSU Archives/ Everett Collection Historical), 45 (© Amoret Tanner), 47 (© Adams Picture Library t/a apl), 55b (© The Print Collector); Baz Richardson p. 29; Capstone Global Library pp. 11, 15, 27, 48 (Tristan Leverett), 37; Corbis 10 (© Kevin Horan), 31 (© ELOY ALONSO/ Reuters), 32 (© Bettmann), 38 (© Chen Kai/Xinhua Press), 39 (© PoodlesRock); Getty Images pp. 4 (Image Source), 13 (Stock Montage/Archive Photos), 17 (Joe Dovala/ WaterFrame); Image Courtesy of The Advertising Archives p. 43; Image of Eastern Woodland Indian Village used with permission of Jefferson Patterson Park & Museum p. 55t; Michael Wall, 55; Nassau County Department of Parks, Recreation and Museums: Garvies Point Museum and Preserve p. 51; Shutterstock pp. 7 (© Gnilenkov Aleksey; © Volodymyr Krasyuk; © Nikodem Nijaki; © Eleonora Kolomiyets; © angelo gilardelli; © Elnur), 24 (© Baloncici), 40 (Sue Honoré); SuperStock pp. 7 (Image Source), 53 (Robert Harding Picture Library), 57 (Design Pics); Topfoto p. 21 (The Granger Collection).

Cover photograph: Purple Heart reproduced with the permission of Getty Images (Gary Moss Photography/ Brand X Pictures); woman using smart phone reproduced with the permission of Shutterstock (© bloomua); vintage pocket watch reproduced with the permission of Shutterstock (© cosma); Elephant toy reproduced with the permission of Capstone Global Library (Tristan Leverett). Every effort has been made to contact copyright holders of material reproduced in this book. Any omissions will be rectified in subsequent printings if notice is given to the publisher.

CONTENTS

Some words are shown in **bold,** like this. You can find out what they mean by looking in the glossary.

ALL OUR THINGS AROUND US

It is first thing in the morning, and the alarm on your mobile phone goes off. You stick some music on your CD player, check your emails on your laptop, then pull on your school clothes. In your room, your possessions are all around you. The clothes, phone, video games, jewellery, computer, and MP3 players might not seem like anything special, but all these things were designed by someone, manufactured, and sold in order to become yours. Their history started before you owned them.

Some of your modern communication and media technology belongings are the result of the modern scientific revolution that really got going over 150 years ago. When you text a friend or send them a photo, your phone is using some of the discoveries first developed for the **space race** and use in 20th-century high-tech weapons!

These young people carry many of their possessions around with them. Over a lifetime, a person acquires – and gets rid of – thousands of different possessions.

Possessions have history

All the things people have owned and used have a history. Looking at your own possessions and those of your family keeps you in touch with the past, even your own childhood. Research into the belongings people have surrounded themselves with through time helps us to understand more about history. The history of an object has many aspects:

- Physical make-up: All your possessions are made out of something. For example, lots of furniture is made out of wood. Other materials, such as some metals, glass, and plastics, have been used more recently. Changes and advances in scientific knowledge and technical skills cause an increase in certain materials. Possessions in particular styles, materials, or even certain colours become popular and then go out of fashion. Over time, **mass-produced** factory goods have become more common than individual items created by craftsmen.

- Use and need: Some objects are developed and used because there is a need for them. In a very cold climate, people tend to have specific possessions that will help to keep them warm, such as coats made of warm fabrics, thick bedding, and close-fitting hats. In a warm climate, the needs are different and include sandals, sunhats, and fans.

- Social, political, and economic change: Over time, changes in the ways people live affect what belongings they have. For example, in the past when few women worked outside of the home, most of their possessions were **domestic**, relating to their lives as mothers, wives, or household servants. Many objects could be identified as being owned by either men or women. The possessions people own also change as populations become more educated, gain political power, such as the right to vote, or have more money to spend. If they have more **disposable income**, people buy things they want rather than just things they need. These possessions might be for leisure or fun and not have any practical use.

Zoom in: Space age specs

Do your glasses or sunglasses have scratch-resistant lenses? If they do, then the technology behind your possession has benefited from the space race. Non-scratch plastic lenses were developed for the helmet visors of US astronauts.

Finding out about your possessions

Every possession can be researched to discover information about how and why it was made. Sometimes it will even be possible to trace all the owners of an object, particularly if it has been a family heirloom. You will need to look for **reliable evidence**. Evidence is anything you can discover and examine that tells you about the object you are researching. It comes in many different forms, from books to newspapers to letters and photographs.

A **primary source** is a piece of evidence from the time in history when something happened, for example, a family photograph which shows a possession, such as a Victorian mantle clock. It can also be written by the person involved in an autobiography (a story of somebody's life written by the person). When the evidence is produced later, for example, a resource book about the different models of 19th-century timepieces, then it is a **secondary source**.

All evidence needs to be **evaluated** for its importance and reliability. Does the photograph really show the clock that is still in the family? How can you be sure? If it has been passed down through several generations, and is even listed as a **bequest** in a family **will**, then you can be pretty certain it is the same clock. When you have a proven history of ownership for an object, the term used for this is its **provenance**.

Where should I look?

Someone invented or designed all of your possessions. You could use an internet search engine to find out about the people behind the history of some of your belongings. For example, if you research the term "video game", you will learn that *Spacewar!* was one of the first popular modern video games, and that Steve Russell was its developer. You could find out more about him, such as his educational background and whether he has designed other games. You can also locate interesting historical information about your possessions by browsing sites that list inventors and their inventions. This site covers inventors, designers, and engineers: **www.spartacus.schoolnet.co.uk/engineers.htm**

These hats show how the fashions and materials used for hats have changed over time and over different cultures. In the centre is the baseball cap, which was first used over 100 years ago as part of a player's uniform. It is now worn by millions of people, male and female, young and old, who have never played baseball. In 2012, a 1920s cap once worn by American baseball legend Ty Cobb sold for $253,000 (around £167,000)!

Zoom in: What are heirlooms?

Heirlooms are the possessions passed down through several generations of a family. These heirlooms, or family treasures, include photographs, pieces of furniture, and items of jewellery. An heirloom does not need to have a great age, such as an **antique**, or a high financial value. Its value is in the connection to specific family members or family memories.

FROM TEDDY'S BEAR TO TEDDY BEAR

For his first birthday in 1921, an English boy was given a stuffed toy teddy bear. His parents bought it at the London department store, Harrods. As he got a bit older, the little boy, Christopher Robin Milne, called his much-loved toy "Edward Bear". Christopher's father was the writer A.A. Milne, and he started to write stories featuring his son's toy. By the time the first story was published in the mid-1920s, Christopher had changed his bear's name to "Winnie-the-Pooh".

Bear facts

A stuffed toy may be one of a person's earliest possessions, and many people secretly treasure them when they are older. It is easy to trace the history of Christopher Robin's toy because it became, and still is, one of the most famous teddy bears ever to have existed. From the time it was purchased in 1921 until today, its history has been recorded. Since 1987, the original Winnie-the-Pooh bear, as well as Christopher Milne's other stuffed toys – Piglet, Kanga, Eeyore, and Tigger – have been on display at the New York Public Library.

Your favourite childhood possession might not be famous like Christopher Robin Milne's Winnie-the-Pooh, but it is still possible to do research and make a record of its history.

But even ordinary early childhood possessions have a history. Here are some simple ways to find out about a toy or game that is yours, or one that belonged to a parent or grandparent.

- Ask family members what they remember about the toy, for example, when it first came into the family, who it belonged to, and if it had a name. If it was a gift, find out whom it came from. If it was purchased, does anyone remember where it was from and if the shop still exists?

- Examine the toy. If you are lucky, it will have a label or tag. If it is wood, plastic, or metal, it might have a model number, **patent** number, or country of origin printed on it or inscribed somewhere. These details can sometimes be used to date an item.

- Check online to see if you can get more information about the company that made the toy or the shop that sold it. Look at auction sites to see if the toy is rare or valuable.

- You can use the information you have gathered to make a provenance record card for the object. This can be a paper record or a computer **document**. You can even take photos to attach to the record.

Where should I look?

There are many places where you can find out about the history of toys and games. Some items, like teddy bears, dolls, and toy soldiers, are important enough to have had many things written about them. Try these websites for information about toy inventors and manufacturers, and for timelines following the development of indoor and outdoor toys and games:

- **www.toyhalloffame.org** – Website of a museum in the state of New York in the US, which holds many historical examples of toys and games.

- **www.bbc.co.uk/schools/primaryhistory/victorian_britain/ toys_and_games** – A highly interactive website featuring pictures, videos, quizzes and examples of activities around toys both old and new.

- **www.ideafinder.com/history/category/toys.htm** – This site features key dates in the history of toys and games, as well as links and information about other resources to find out more.

Curios to collectables

For several hundred years, people have collected things that they found interesting or thought might be valuable. Early explorers, travellers, and individuals interested in science developed collections relating to their interests, from art to insects to rocks and fossils. These were often displayed for friends or just kept for the collector's personal enjoyment. The collecting of **curios** became massively popular in the 19th century, with rich and even middle-class collectors keeping their favourite items in specially made curio cabinets.

In the 20th century, product manufacturers started the trend for including collectable items with their goods. This started with cards of sportsmen included with packets of cigarettes and spread to other products.

Zoom in: Creating limited editions of toys

Ty Warner (pictured below) of Ty Co took it a step further when he created the collectable soft toys known as Beanie Babies. These became popular in the 1990s. These small stuffed animals were each given a name and birth date when they were introduced. They were made in **limited editions** and were only sold for a short time. This made people very keen to get new animals before they were no longer available. The resale values of some Beanie Babies were very high and collectors became obsessed with getting the rare ones.

Object	stuffed toy elephant
Description	worn grey plush fabric with red limb ends, plastic eyes, and small white fabric tag, 38 cm long
Style	cute, cartoon-style, not realistic
Date acquired	around 16 March 1957
Name given	Ellie Elephant
Origin	not known
Manufacturing details	very worn tag says Jumbo Gund, other details hard to read
Any other information	was a present for owner's brother when he was born in March 1957, and then "given" by the baby to his five-year-old sister

An information record like this, for a well-loved possession, can record details that might be lost or forgotten. For valuable items, such as jewellery, some insurance companies require that owners keep details and photos in case they want to make a claim.

Research roadshow: Theodore Roosevelt and the young bear

The teddy bear has only been a child's toy for just over 100 years. It owes its existence to a US president who could not bring himself to shoot a young black bear. President Theodore Roosevelt (in office 1901–1909), known as Teddy, went on a hunting trip in the US state of Mississippi in 1902. During the hunt, he was asked to shoot a bear that had been chased to exhaustion and then tied up. Roosevelt felt it was very unsportsmanlike to shoot a bound animal and so refused. The bear was severely injured, and was later killed to put it out of its misery, but the story spread about Teddy Roosevelt sparing the young bear. There were newspaper articles and cartoons drawn to recount the story.

Soon after this, two sets of toy designers, Rose and Morris Michtom in the United States and Richard Steiff in Germany, designed stuffed toy bears that they called "teddy bears", after Roosevelt. Both men went on to work for very successful toy companies. Morris Michtom founded the Ideal Novelty and Toy Company. It is now owned by Mattel and Hasbro. The Steiff Company produced many types of teddy bears and other stuffed toys. Some are now very valuable and sought after by teddy bear collectors. In 2010, an early Steiff teddy bear sold for £18,750! The Steiff Company is still in business after more than 130 years.

Zoom in: The Steiff ear button

There are many places you can look on the internet or in books to see photos of stuffed toys produced in Germany by the Steiff Company. One way to check if a toy is an original Steiff creation is to look for the special metal ear button firmly attached to one ear of all Steiff animals from 1904. This was to help buyers identify a real Steiff bear from imitations. The early metal buttons had the image of an elephant impressed in them. Later, the word "Steiff" replaced the elephant. Collectors today have to be very careful when they buy old Steiff animals, as fake ear buttons are sometimes attached to other old bears.

DRAWING
THE LINE
IN MISSISSIPPI

Berryman 1902

This political cartoon (which originally appeared in *The Washington Post* in 1902) depicts the US president of the time, Theodore Roosevelt, refusing to shoot a small bear (shown in the background, being restrained). Roosevelt's nickname was Teddy. Partly thanks to this cartoon, and the press coverage around the incident, the first stuffed toy bears called teddy bears were then produced and sold.

CHINA FROM CHINA: BLUE, WHITE, AND PRECIOUS

Storms whip up very quickly in the channels between the islands of Indonesia. A wooden ship caught in one storm was heavily loaded with goods. After it had hit a reef and water was pouring in, it sank to the bottom of the sea. The year was 1752, and the *Geldermalsen* and its cargo (the items carried on the ship) would not be seen again for over 230 years.

Treasure hunters and explorers

In 1986, Michael Hatcher found the Dutch East India Company ship *Geldermalsen* off the coast of the Indonesian Lingga Islands. When it sank in 1752, it was travelling between Canton (now called Guangzhou) and the Netherlands with a cargo of china, tea, and gold. Hatcher is a member of a group of **maritime** explorers that some people call treasure hunters. They look for shipwrecks from the past. By selling the valuable items they find, or even the ships themselves, they finance future expeditions. Hatcher discovered and salvaged nearly 150,000 pieces of china from the wreck. At an auction in Amsterdam in 1986, this china, now called the "Nanking cargo", made over £10 million!

Canton to Lingga to Amsterdam to England

Museums and wealthy collectors purchased some of the biggest, most important, and rarest pieces of the Nanking cargo. However, there were also many small, more affordable pieces in the cargo. Over the years since the auction, many people have found themselves the proud owners of one or two pieces.

Stephen Redfern did not buy his piece of the cargo in the original sale. He saw it advertised 25 years later on an internet auction site. It was easy to trace the small blue and white bowl's history, because it had only one owner since the Amsterdam sale. Stephen loved the idea of owning something at least 260 years old that had spent most of its life in a wreck on the seabed. As a history teacher, he also liked having a possession that had been sold on one of the great **trade routes** of the 18th century. You can research more about the growth of trade by looking at topics such as the Silk Road, the spice trade, the Dutch East Indies Company, and the Hanseatic League.

Stephen, who lives in Oxfordshire, likes the idea of using his small blue and white Nanking cargo bowl, even though it is so old. It was made to be household china to be used every day, so using it to eat rice, cereal, or ice cream is totally appropriate. However, as it is so delicate, valuable, and old, it can't go in the dishwasher afterwards!

Where should I look?

You can research more about salvage hunters online. Find out more about Michael Hatcher and his life as the most famous seeker after sunken treasure by reading Hugh Edwards' biography *Treasures of the Deep: The Extraordinary Life and Times of Captain Mike Hatcher* (HarperCollins, 2000).

There are also many articles and blogs online about Mike, some positive and some negative. In 2012, Captain Hatcher sold off most of his own personal collection of treasures from the 80-plus wrecks he has salvaged. You can check the internet for the newspaper coverage about this amazing auction.

Making a connection: Archaeology versus salvage

Salvagers and treasure hunters like Michael Hatcher often find themselves at odds with historians and archaeologists (those who recover and study historical things). This happened with the search for, discovery, and recovery of items from the *Geldermalsen*. Those who want to protect historical **heritage** were angered by what had happened.

Below are some points people make for and against maritime salvage hunters and their ways of discovering and dealing with historical objects.

Note that some objects from wrecks are historically interesting, but not worth much money if sold. Because they are not "treasure", salvagers sometimes do not even bother to retrieve them from sites. Which side is right, or do both positions make reasonable points?

For salvage hunters

- There are so many wrecks that won't be discovered unless these people search for them.

- The things found by salvagers and treasure hunters go onto the sale market so museums and private collectors can buy them for display. This is no different from how most items end up in museums.

- Salvage hunters use some of their profits to upgrade the technological specifications of their search vessels. Most governments and university archaeology departments cannot afford to have the specialist, up-to-date equipment that is necessary to survey the oceans and seas for wrecks.

Against salvage hunters

- Treasure hunters only care about the monetary value of the objects they find on a wreck. They don't look at the **context** of the things they find, or the historical information they can learn from the ships themselves.

- When treasure hunters sell the objects they find, the objects may end up far away from the place they were found or made. The heritage of a local area, particularly if it is too poor to pay international auction prices, can suffer if items from its past are spread around the world.

- Most wrecks are also the graves of the crews and passengers who went down with the ships. People worry that wreck sites will not be treated with respect.

This diver is recovering items from a wreck found off Micronesia in the Pacific Ocean.

Golden treasure on the *Geldermalsen*

Although the thousands of pieces of Chinese **porcelain** salvaged from the wreck are now spread around the world in museums and in private collections, such as Stephen's bowl, there was also true treasure in the ship – 125 rare pure gold bars (also known as ingots). Most of them were sold at the Amsterdam auction in 1986. There was great interest in these objects, since they were the first Chinese 18th century gold items sold to Western collectors. Some of the gold was in normal, rectangular bars, while others were unique cup-shaped ingots, called "Nanking shoes".

What is blue and white porcelain?

Today, we use the word "china" for most dishes and crockery, particularly items made of porcelain. Did you know that this is because, for many years, all the porcelain dishes in the world came from China? The Chinese had a special way of making them and guarded this secret method very closely. This made Chinese porcelain very valuable and sought after. Unlike the pottery-based crockery available in Europe, porcelain was much finer and more delicate. Millions of pieces of porcelain from China travelled to the Middle East and Europe on the trade routes from Asia.

One of the most popular designs for the porcelain pieces exported from China is now known as "blue and white". This name describes many different patterns where there is a blue pictorial design on a white background. Most of the Nanking cargo china is blue and white. Europeans in the Netherlands and in England eventually worked out how to make crockery that looked like porcelain, and then to actually make porcelain. Try researching topics like hard paste porcelain, Delftware, and the Willow pattern to find out more about European china.

Eating off history

Everyone owns dishes they use regularly for meals, but some people own more decorative china or **inherited** family pieces. To find out more about any porcelain or pottery that your family owns, read the information printed on the base. On pieces made in the last 150 years or so, you will see the country of origin listed as well as the name of the company and probably the name or number of the pattern. Older Chinese or Japanese porcelain might only have characters in those languages. Early European porcelain might only have initials or a mark, such as the symbol of crossed swords for the Meissen factory in Germany.

Zoom in: The Willow pattern

One of the most famous blue and white china decoration designs is called the "Willow pattern". But this pattern was never used on Chinese porcelain. It was designed by British porcelain maker Thomas Minton in the late 18th century. The inspiration for the design was the romantic stories that images on Chinese porcelain often showed.

The forming of trade routes

The map below shows the general directions of trade trips over the centuries. It is difficult to show specific routes, as these have changed.

For thousands of years people from one place have bartered, exchanged, or sold items to people from other places. This could be between areas close to each other or over long distances. When trade journeys between areas followed the same path, these became known as trade routes.

Many of the trade routes were identified with the items that moved along them. The Silk Road was an early overland trade route that was popular between the 7th century and the 12th century. It brought the luxury fabric silk between China in the Far East, where it was made, and the Middle East and Europe, where it could be sold for very high prices.

Another of the most important and profitable trade routes was the Spice Route. Spices, such as pepper, cinnamon, and ginger, were sought after in Europe and the Middle East for their use in flavouring, preserving food, and medicine. These spices grew in areas to the east of the Indian Ocean. They had to be purchased and then transported by land and sea over thousands of miles. During some periods in medieval Europe, pepper was so rare and highly prized that it was worth more than the same weight in gold! Spice traders and merchants became very rich!

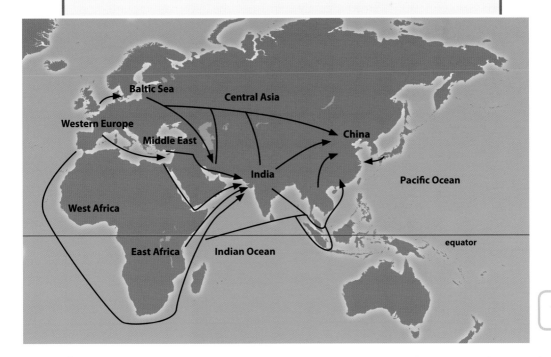

THE MODEL T FORD: ANY COLOUR SO LONG AS IT'S BLACK

In 1935, a man from New York state drove his car to the US capital, Washington DC, but he went back home without it. It was a 1913 Model T Ford, and the man, Harvey Carlton Locke, had donated his prized possession to be an exhibit at a famous national museum, the Smithsonian Institution.

Already an icon

Why would a car that was only 22 years old and still in working order be considered a museum exhibit? However much you might love your old bike or skateboard, it is unlikely a museum would want to put your possessions on display. But Harvey Locke's much-loved Model T Ford was more than just an old car – it was already an example of a transport and lifestyle revolution that changed the world. The history of Harvey's car is also the story of the modern industrialized societies that developed during and after World War I (1914–1918). Harvey's car, and the 15 million other Model T Fords sold between 1908 and 1927, were possessions that changed the world.

From a luxury, to a car for every family

Henry Ford wanted the automobile to be a possession that all hard-working people could aspire to. He needed a good design and a cheap and quick method of production. This would also help keep the sale price low. The answer was a new way of building a complex product like a car – the **assembly line**. The car moved along a pathway while all the parts were quickly fitted, so the time it took to piece together a Model T was reduced to only 93 minutes. The age of mass production had begun. Partly due to this quick system, by 1924, the Model T cost less than a third of what it did when it was originally on sale.

> ### Right and wrong *i*
> It has always been rumoured that Henry Ford said people could have any colour of Model T so long as it was black. In reality, until 1914, Model T Fords were also available in green, red, blue, and grey. It was only after 1914 that they were available only in black.

This 1913 Model T Ford was a much-loved possession of Harvey Carlton Locke. His father, Harvey W. Locke, was a pioneering camera-maker and the car's original purchaser. After the Model T Ford was first introduced in 1908, the lifestyle of those who bought the car, and cars in the future, changed forever.

Zoom in: Why the name "Model T"?

In the early years of the 20th century, when many small automobile manufacturing companies were coming out with their own car designs, the vehicles were not usually given interesting names. They were called things like "Model" or "Type" followed by a number or letter. Car makers had to avoid numbers or letters already used by competitors. So, the "T" in Model T doesn't stand for anything (for example, it is not the twentieth car designed by Henry Ford!).

Cars create demand for more possessions

However, affordable cars were just the beginning. Cars needed roads, motoring accessories, petrol stations, and repair garages. Families driving out into the country at the weekend needed roadside cafes and places to visit. Well-paid car factory workers needed homes to live in and things to buy with their money. The **consumer society** had started.

But were all these advances for the best? Did Ford's new methods just lead to **materialism** and a throwaway culture, based on the easy availability of certain products?

Read the "Making a connection" box on page 23 and create a table that lists the positive and negative points of assembly line mass production. Use the example at the bottom of the box. How easy is it to come to a conclusion here? Does your table have more positive or negative points about the process of mass production?

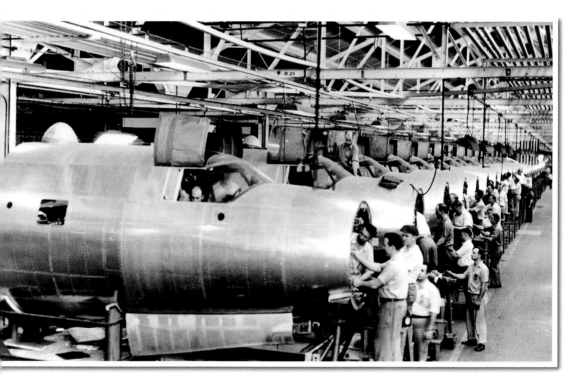

By the time World War II started, those involved realized that the Ford system of a moving assembly line could help quickly to create the **munitions** and other equipment, such as aeroplanes and tanks, needed to fight.

Making a connection: Mass production and the consumer society

So how did Henry Ford and his manufacturing techniques help start the consumer society? Here are a few things to think about:

- The automated assembly lines introduced by Ford were not only used to make affordable cars. The same methods were later transferred to the production of many goods. The assembly style of production meant that items could be made more quickly and that means more cheaply. Mass-produced items cost less than they previously had under the old manufacturing methods. Today, many of your possessions, including CDs, DVDs, and most of the **components** in more complex items like mobile phones, are manufactured using mass production methods.

- Some of the cheaply produced things were made to be replaced more frequently.

- The working conditions in Ford factories were clean and safe. Workers were paid well and therefore had money to spend on their own cars and other consumer goods. However, most workers needed no special skills, and the craftsmanship of the old engineering methods was soon lost.

- The demands of the new consumer society led to higher employment in the mass production factories, as people wanted more and more things.

Can you think of anything else?

Positive	Negative
assembly line mass production is so quick that it keeps prices low on many items.	no one knows how to make anything by hand any more; many old skills have been lost.

Being a motoring collector

People not only buy cars, but they also buy car accessories, toy cars, racing games, and all sorts of car **memorabilia**. Some collectable items, such as badges and old motoring magazines, are not too expensive. Other items, particularly **vintage** cars, can be very expensive, partly because they are so rare.

You might never be able to own a supercar or drive a Formula 1 vehicle, but you can collect model racing cars or try to get signed photos of the drivers. Some people collect items related to early petrol stations and the oil companies that ran them. Motoring guides and maps over 50 years old often turn up in charity shops and jumble sales. These sources tell you a lot about life at the time they were produced.

Dependence on cars has its problems. These include the need for more and bigger roads, and the difficulties of providing cars with fuel. There are also environmental concerns relating to air pollution and the disposal of old cars and tyres.

Where should I look?

Henry Ford became rich and influential during his lifetime, and his company still produces cars all over the world. As well as secondary sources about Ford, such as articles on websites and in encyclopaedias, there is a Henry Ford Museum (**www.hfmgv.org**). The Smithsonian Institution has an official website with many images and details about its motoring exhibits from cars to toolkits (**www.si.edu**).

You can also research other people and vehicles identified with the spread of motoring, such as Alec Issigonis (1906–1988) and the BMC Mini, or Ferdinand Porsche (1875–1951) and the Volkswagen Type I (known as the Beetle). If you have a family car, you can research the company that made it and even the people involved in its design. It might have some features that were once, or still are, innovative. Research terms like hybrid technology, parking sensor, air bag, and catalytic converter.

Zoom in: Ethically-made possessions

Ford's methods of mass production, which also used many interchangeable parts, certainly made products cheaply enough to be able to sell them at low prices. However, many of the factories where items such as mobile phones and MP3 players are made are now based in developing countries. Some of the workers receive very low wages and have to work unrealistic hours in unsafe conditions. Items made in these types of conditions are said to be **unethical**. These factories may use some or all of the following bad practices:
- They use raw materials that are scarce or endangered.
- They do not care about the health and safety of employees.
- They make the employees work very, or unreasonably long hours.
- They use child workers.
- They expect unrealistic numbers of the items to be made every day.
- They pay very low wages.

You could research the manufacturing processes used by some of the companies that make your possessions. Are you happy with how they treat their workers?

DO MEDALS MEAN OUR ANCESTOR WAS IN A WAR?

The stone **memorial** plaque on the wall inside the local church gives the details of Alfred James Cross' short life: he was born in 1898, and he died in 1917 fighting for his country. What it doesn't say is that this was all his grieving parents and nine brothers and sisters had to remember him by. His body was never recovered, so he had no traditional "grave". The plaque and the medals he was awarded became the focus of their memories.

Great-great Uncle Alfie's medals

Leo Arnett had seen the military medals at home in a special box of treasured family possessions. It was not until his sister needed to use them for a school project that he became interested. But he found it hard to think of someone who died at the age of 19 as great-great-uncle Alfred. Leo decided to think of him as Alfie.

Leo started his search for information about the medals and Alfie. His mother advised him to look on the 1911 **census**. Alfie was there, aged 12, living in a village not far from the estate where his father worked as a gamekeeper. This meant that when Alfie **enlisted** near the beginning of the war he was only just old enough, or he lied to get in. The census details and the memorial in the village church helped Leo find Alfie on the casualty lists of World War I.

Brave and distinguished – but no grave

When Leo found Alfie's death record, there was much more information. Alfie had served in the Rifle Brigade of the Prince Consort's Own Regiment, 2nd Battalion. He had been a private when he enlisted, but he was already a sergeant at the time of his death. The most exciting thing was there was a citation, or note, to go with the most important of the three medals the family believed had been awarded to Alfie. Here was the proof of a hero in the family. The British Army's Distinguished Conduct Medal had been issued to Alfred Cross:

> "For conspicuous gallantry and devotion to duty. He led out a patrol and established two posts about 70 yards from an enemy strong point. He set a splendid example of courage and initiative."

Alfred James Cross received several medals. One is the campaign medal given to everyone who fought in World War I. Another is a medal that was awarded to all who died in action. The Distinguished Conduct Medal is the most important. It means that Alfred was a hero. It is the medal in the top left with the red and dark blue ribbon.

Zoom in: The trenches – mud, blood, and death

World War I is remembered for the mud in the defences known as trenches, and the huge numbers of those killed in the massive battles, such as Ypres where Alfie died. You can find out more about what life was like in the trenches by researching key terms such as trench foot, frontline, shell shock, and No Man's Land.

Pinned on with pride

Military medals in some form have existed for armies and other fighting forces around the world since the time of Alexander the Great in the 4th century BC. However, it was not until the 19th century that the first medals were given to everyone who fought in a certain battle. The British soldiers who fought in the Battle of Waterloo in 1815 were the first to receive a medal like this.

During the Crimean War (1853–1856), other British medals were introduced, including the Victoria Cross, known as the VC (1856, for all ranks), and the Distinguished Conduct Medal (1854, for non-commisioned officers and other ranks). In the US, local commanders started awarding medals during the American Civil War (1861–1865). The only one of these still being awarded is one of the most important – the Medal of Honor. The US military services started awarding medals centrally during the Spanish-American War (1898) when the first campaign medal was awarded to all who fought.

Where should I look?

All members of the military have a personal service record. This should list any medals awarded. Information about units and regiments can be found in military **logbooks** and war diaries, and the **dispatches** sent back from war zones.

The Imperial War Museum (**www.iwm.org.uk**) and the National Army Museum (**www.nam.ac.uk**) can be visited in person or online. Most of the historic British army regiments have regimental associations with museums. These will have displays of uniforms and medals. Try searching **www.armymuseums.org.uk**

For information about military possessions, such as medals and uniforms, look online at sites that sell them. This could include auction sites. The photographs and descriptions are usually very good and you can look without buying!

Not all military items are weapons. This drum, from the time of England's war with Spain in the 16th century, is an early example of a military instrument. From bugles to bagpipes, for hundreds of years armies have liked accompanying the sounds of war with music.

Research roadshow: Collecting the military past

Some people collect things related to the military (called militaria), and they usually do it in one of three ways:

- They collect a class of items, such as cap badges or flags.
- They collect everything from a particular war or a battle within a war.
- They collect everything to do with a particular regiment, battalion, ship, or flying squadron.

Online auction sites tell you how much items sell for. Use them to find out the value of your own collection (or a fair price). There are often fairs selling militaria. You can arrange trades and sales at these fairs or with other collectors you meet, or through social media.

DYNATAC: TALKING ON A BRICK

On the street corner, a queue of people stood outside the telephone box waiting for a chance to make their calls. Then a well-dressed young man paused by those waiting and reached into his briefcase for a rectangular white box the size of a house brick. After straightening the aerial, he punched his number into a keypad on the box and spoke into it while walking away in the sunshine. It was 1983 and this was the start of what would become a communications revolution.

No longer tied to wires

If you saw the object in the picture on page 31, what would you think of it? Maybe you have seen a similar chunky, old mobile phone in the back of a drawer or bottom of a wardrobe at home. It might look very old-fashioned now, but this was in at the start of a radical change in communications. This is the device that ultimately led to telephone calls "on the go", to and from nearly any place in the world!

Previously, telephone users relied on telephones at fixed points connected by wires – landlines. Then, in 1983, the Motorola DynaTAC 8000X, the first really portable hand-held mobile phone, hit the market. These early wireless mobiles were not affordable for the average person, and they could only be used for about half an hour before they needed 10 hours of recharging.

A technological explosion

Since the introduction of the early "brick" phones, as they became known, the speed of change and development in mobile communications has been huge. New models of **cellular-digital** handsets were almost out of date as soon as they were bought. As the competition hotted up, prices fell and more and more people, including some children, became mobile phone users. Modern smartphones can be smaller, are a lot thinner, and are far more advanced than the DynaTAC. They are far more powerful and have many more features than the most advanced laptop computers from the end of the 20th century! For example, they often have integrated GPS (Global Positioning Satellite) technology, which can help you to navigate your way to a place.

The first mobile phone
Model: DynaTAC 8000X
Maker: Motorola Company
Talk-time: 30 minutes
Size: 330 x 45 x 88 mm
(13 by 1¾ by 3½ in.)
Weight: 790 g (28 oz.)
Produced: 1983–1986
Original sale price: US$3,995

This is the Motorola DynaTAC 8000X, which was introduced in 1983. People now laugh and call the DynaTAC and similar mobile phones "bricks", but in the early 1980s they were at the cutting edge of communications technology. The man shown in this 2009 photograph is Dr Martin Cooper, one of the men who developed the phone for Motorola.

Zoom in: Money in mobiles

When people bought the first mobile phone "bricks", they were a luxury item that only the well-off could afford. But the first mobile phone models, even though they were very old-fashioned technologically, are still worth a lot of money. Only 30 years old, they are now collectors' items and even appear in museum displays. In 2011, a rare DynaTAC 8000X sold on an internet auction site for over £900. Other old mobile phones, even ones that are not rare, are now collectable. Mobile phone collectors have online newsletters and blogs.

The telephone backstory

The landline system developed when Scottish-American scientist and inventor Alexander Graham Bell obtained a patent for his first telephone in 1876. Telephone networks quickly spread throughout the United States and other developed countries. By 1960, there were 240 million connected telephone lines worldwide.

Father of the mobile phone

Alexander Graham Bell's work on the development of the telephone is well known. However, few people have heard of John F. Mitchell of the Motorola Company, but he could be called the "father" of the mobile phone. Along with his colleague Dr Martin Cooper, he engineered and then championed the cause of portable wireless communication. His work led to the birth of the commercial hand-held mobile phone with the DynaTAC 8000X in 1983.

Starting in the 1960s with transistor pagers, John F. Mitchell was involved in all aspects of the invention and patenting of mobile and wireless technology. Mitchell is shown here in the 1970s with a DynaTAC prototype.

What are all the Gs?

The different technological stages of mobile phones are called 1G, 2G, 3G, 4G, and 5G. The G stands for "generation", meaning stage of development.

1G – These were the first analogue cellular phones from the 1980s.

2G – In 1991, the second generation of mobiles used digital, rather than analogue, technology.

3G – Smartphones represent the third generation of mobile phone technology. They can connect to broadband internet.

4G – New standards for faster and more reliable broadband network connections have created the fourth generation.

5G – The fifth generation will vastly increase data download speeds.

Recording the recent oral history of the telephone

Everyone takes portable communication for granted now. Because the introduction and growth of the mobile phone market has occurred in the last 30 years, these possessions are a good subject for **oral history** research.

Oral history research involves interviewing people about the past. Talk to friends, family, and teachers about their experiences with telephones. Older people can talk about their early experiences with landline telephones.

You can take notes of their responses or preferably record your interviews. It can also be useful to get all your interviewees to fill in questionnaires. This way you can get extra details and make sure that everyone has answered the same questions. Questions prepared beforehand can get people to talk, they could have things to say you haven't thought about! Here are a few sample questions you might use in a questionnaire:

• Do you think students should be allowed to bring mobile phones to school and use them during school time?

• Are you more interested in all the things a phone can do, or how cool or popular the model is?

• Can you imagine a world that is once again without mobile phones? What would you miss most?

Avoid questions that can be answered with a simple "Yes" or "No" response.

THE VINDOLANDA POSTCARDS: KEEPING IN TOUCH

"I have sent you … pairs of socks from Sattua, two pairs of sandals and two pairs of underpants… Greet … Elpis … Tetrius and all your messmates with whom I pray that you live in the greatest good fortune." This old postcard sent to a soldier far away from home shows how worried his family were about him. But this man was not serving in Afghanistan or the Middle East. This soldier was with his unit of the Roman Army at an isolated outpost in northern Britain, and it was around AD 100.

The urge to communicate

Maybe the anonymous soldier received his parcel from home, but a lot could have happened to it on the journey. Nowadays, when a family wants to get in touch with serving military personnel halfway around the world, it is much simpler with texting, email, webcam chat services, or the more old-fashioned option of a letter or postcard.

Messages from the past

This soldier's message from home is part of the collection of handwritten **Latin** documents called the Vindolanda tablets. These are up to 1,600 thin pieces of wood, about the size of a postcard, with various messages on them in ink. Some are letters to and from family and friends, while others relate to official military correspondence and camp business. The first tablets were discovered during archaeological investigations in 1973 at the Vindolanda military campsite in the north of England, and more turn up every year as the area is explored or excavated. When the soldier lost or threw away his possession, he left us evidence of something very important about human relationships; it shows people have always wanted to keep in touch.

From wood and ink to paper and ink

Since the Vindolanda tablets were sent and received, there have been improvements in the reliability of message carrying. This is due to government involvement in organizing postal services, advances in transport, and international co-operation. To find out more, try researching key words such as Pony Express, Royal Mail, telegraph, Morse code, and airmail.

Where should I look?

You can see the Vindolanda tablets and read the English translations on many websites and in books. Here are a few suggestions for further research:

• **www.vindolanda.com**
The Vindolanda Trust website has lots of information about the tablets and life in an ancient Roman military camp.

• **www.bbc.co.uk/history/ancient/romans/vindolanda_01.shtml**
This site ties quotes from the tablets with information about various aspects of life for the soldiers of the Roman Empire.

Possessions like the Vindolanda tablets, rediscovered after thousands of years, can show us differences and similarities between the past and the present. Methods of correspondence have changed out of all recognition in 2,000 years. However, the text on these primary sources focuses on many of the same things that people still write and talk about today: family ties, affection, money, food, health, and social status.

Postal memorabilia

Many people keep old correspondence, usually letters and postcards. A careful look at any written communications you find can tell you a lot about their history. For example, postcards can be examined in several ways:

- First, the physical make-up of the postcard can be investigated. What kind of paper is it made of: shiny or matte? Can the size give you any clues about its age? If it is a picture postcard, is it personal, such as a photograph of a family member, or is it a commercially produced image with a caption on the card?

- Second, the stamp and postmark can tell you a lot. Different designs and values of stamps were in use at certain dates. Is it a local stamp or one from another country? If it is clear enough to read, the postmark will give you the place and date when the card was sent. During some periods, the postmark even gave the exact time the correspondence was processed!

- Third, the message can be very informative. You can see if the person the card is addressed to is a family member. If so, not only the content of the writing on the card, but the handwriting itself could be interesting.

Research roadshow: Detective work on an old family postcard

Julie Arnett found many old letters and postcards when helping to clear out an elderly relative's house. Most were 80 to 100 years old, but one in particular caught her eye. It seemed quite mysterious and she didn't understand the message. She decided to investigate. She had a few things to go on. The stamp had fallen off, but there was a postmark. Julie could see it had been sent from Peterborough. Then there was the address the card was sent to. She went online and used a **genealogy** website to check the census returns for the early 1900s to see who lived there and if any names were familiar. This helped her work out that the card had been sent from a brother to his sister while he was working away from home. From what she knew about her family tree, Julie realized that they were actually her great-great-uncle and great-grandmother!

POST CARD

THE ADDRESS TO BE WRITTEN ON THIS SIDE.

STAMP HERE.

Mrs L Archer

25 Broadway

West Front, Exeter Cathedral

Julie thinks she has puzzled out the mysteries of her inherited postcard. Have a look at the old correspondence in your house to see if there is any research you could do. Don't forget to look at the stamps!

Zoom in: Starting a postcard collection

If you want to collect postal memorabilia, postcards are a cheap and interesting place to start. You could look in charity shops, second-hand shops, and online. You could collect using a theme, such as old images of a particular location. Maybe you'll be lucky and find a family collection you can build on.

Cost a penny, but worth millions

Have a look at the old stamps on family letters and postcards. The very first UK and US stamps from the 1840s, such as "Penny Blacks", "Twopenny Blues", "5 cent Benjamin Franklins", and "10 cent George Washingtons" are all very rare and worth large amounts of money. In 2011, a "Twopenny" sold for £1 million!

Although you are very unlikely to find any stamps that are old or valuable, many households have stamp collections or first day covers. First day covers are special stamps postmarked on the first day they were issued. They usually celebrate the life of a famous person or commemorate a famous event. You can research the people and events, or try to find out more about the way the stamps are designed and produced. The study of stamps and stamp collecting has been a popular hobby for over 150 years. This pastime is known as philately. There are also people who search for interesting and rare postmarks, cancellation stampings, and other postal markings. This hobby is called marcophily or marcophilately.

This postman is delivering mail in a remote mountainous region of southwest China using a pony. It is still the only way to get post to people in an area like this.

The Pony Express system served a need when other forms of transporting post and important messages were not available. Telegraph, rail, and road systems superseded it. Maybe new electronic means of communication will lead to the end of postal services that are already losing money. What some people call "snail mail" is already starting to disappear in many parts of the world.

Zoom in: What was the Pony Express?

The Pony Express was a short-lived, but very fast and efficient, method of delivering post in the Old West of the United States before the telegraph and the transcontinental railway. From April 1860 to October 1861, along a route from St Joseph, Missouri to Sacramento, California, small riders on small horses (not ponies) rode in 16–24 kilometre (10–15 mile) relays. The trail took the riders over mountain ranges and through deserts for 3,164 kilometres (1,966 miles). The goal was to take only 10 days for the entire distance, and the deliveries were almost always on time. During the 18-month operation, only one postal delivery was lost before making it to its destination. Find out more about the Pony Express service and why it came to an end by looking at the websites of the Pony Express Museum (**www.ponyexpress.org**) and the US National Park Service Pony Express Trail (**www.nps.gov/poex**).

TELLING TIME THROUGH TIME

At the beginning of World War II (fought between 1939 and 1945), many children in English cities were evacuated to safer places. Sue's dad knew he was luckier than many of his friends who had been sent to live with strangers. Up north with his aunt and uncle, he and his mother were safe from all the problems in London. It didn't seem like much of a risk when they had to go south again to stay at his grandmother's house while he took his apprenticeship examinations. But it was 14 November 1940 and he was in Coventry. Bombs were falling, and the city was on fire.

The Coventry "Blitz"

Luckily, no one in the house was killed, although an estimated 554 people lost their lives that night. The clock standing in the hallway of the house in Coventry fell over, but didn't hit anybody. Around 450 German bombers arrived, damaging or destroying two-thirds of Coventry's buildings, including the medieval cathedral of St Michael. The family clock, like Sue's dad, survived the Coventry Blitz with only a few bangs and scrapes. This clock is now with its third generation of the family. This possession has a fascinating past.

Sue now has the clock that survived the Coventry Blitz in her own house. Like many family possessions that people keep, it is not a particularly valuable item in itself. What makes this clock precious are the memories of that night in Coventry over 70 years ago. Many people died that night and most of those who survived the bombs and fires are now also gone. The clock's history helps keep their story alive.

Saving time

From the early 19th century when ordinary people could first afford timepieces, they became something that families held onto. The tall standing clocks, known as grandfather or grandmother clocks, were status symbols. The better the clockmaker you purchased your clock from, the better the internal **movement** would be and the more likely it was to tell the time accurately. Clock faces could be plain or very ornate and decorated. The cases could be made of cheap wood or expensive, imported timber, such as mahogany. Later in the century, mantle clocks, made to go on the shelf or surround above a fireplace, became very popular, and large wall clocks started appearing in offices and public places, such as railway stations.

Time in your pocket and on your wrist

You can argue that the most personal way of keeping time is through a watch. From the pocket watches of the 19th and early 20th centuries to the wristwatches of today, watches became something special to individuals. They were given as gifts, for graduations, special birthdays, or retirement. Often, they were inscribed.

Eventually, mass-production and the use of interchangeable parts turned watches from handmade to factory-produced. Even so, any watch owned by a person has an intimate connection with that individual. When you put on a wristwatch worn by a grandparent you know it touched his or her arm like it is now touching yours.

Zoom in: Waving goodbye to the watch?

Today many people have stopped wearing wristwatches. They can check the time on their mobile phones or tablets when they are on the move. This particularly applies to younger people, who have been brought up with this technology. Because of this, watchmakers are trying to compete with mobile phones and tablets by creating apps for watches. Soon watches that are also mobile phones will be widely available. However, expensive watches that are identified with luxury and success have seen an increase in sales since 2011 despite the world-wide financial problems.

Striking, chimes, and alarms

When a large standing clock was the only way to find out the time in a house, there needed to be a way to know the time without having to rush around to look at it. This was especially the case at night when it was dark and you would have to light a candle and go downstairs! For this reason, clocks were made to strike every quarter hour and then strike the same number of times as the hour on the hour, for example, three strikes at three o'clock in the afternoon. Mantle clocks could also strike the hour, but many of them had fancier and more complex chimes.

The "Westminster chimes" is the best known striking clock. It copies the sound made by the clock popularly called Big Ben, which is at the top of a tower at Westminster, London. In fact, it was the bell, which produces the chime, that was originally nicknamed Big Ben. However, the name is now generally used for the clock itself.

Clocks to wake people up in the morning started to come into fashion in the 19th century. The first patent for an alarm clock was issued in 1847 to the French inventor Antoine Reider. However, his model and the later US "tin-can" alarm clock were still quite large and unwieldy. It was only after the American clock company Seth Thomas devised a small bedside alarm clock in the 1870s that they really became popular.

Research roadshow: Clare's watch – fit for royalty

When Clare decided to do some research into her antique pocket watch, she already knew it was quite old, but she had no idea where the story would take her, or the amazing connections she would discover. Like almost all pocket watches, Clare's early 19th-century watch had the maker's name inscribed on it. Using **trade directories**, and other primary sources from the time, Clare was able to find out about the watchmakers. It turned out that the same watchmakers, Mayo & Clark, were supposed to have made a gold pocket watch for Caroline, wife of King George IV. There was no record of what had happened to this watch. Clare's detective work led her to believe that it probably did still exist. The watch was found at Windsor Castle, one of the homes of the current royal family! Clare's watch might not have been owned by royalty, but the connection makes its history much more interesting.

Clocks and watches with digital displays first became available in the early 1970s. They seemed modern and suitable for the new "space age". Everybody wanted one. The technology was very advanced. They used quartz movements driven by electronic pulses from a one-cell replaceable battery.

Where should I look?

It should be quite easy to find out about interesting clocks or watches in your family's possession. Most have the name of the maker or manufacturer on them. There are two names if different people made the movement and the case. Many catalogues, lists, and trade directories survive from the 19th and 20th centuries that contain details about the makers and retailers of clocks and watches. Some big watch companies have their own historical information online. There are clock and watch experts, known as horologists, who have websites and have written books about their interests. There are also specialist collectors' fairs and shops where you can find information and get valuations. Looking online at auction websites is often a good way to find out the value of a watch or clock.

MRS BLOOMER'S BLOOMERS

The woman walked down the street in a stylish but comfortable outfit. The loose trousers under her overskirt and waistcoat meant she could see her feet to walk comfortably on the uneven road surface. But although she seemed perfectly ordinary, the group of small boys passing pointed and laughed before running off. A couple nearby turned and stared at her in shock and surprise. It was 1850. To them, Amelia Bloomer looked like a freak.

From her name to her clothing

Each garment, from the rough animal skins worn by early humans to "smart" jackets that can recharge your mobile phone and MP3 player, has a history. When you get dressed in the morning, the possessions you wear, from your underwear to your coat to your shoes, have changed over time. Today, we identify the name "bloomers" with large, baggy underpants. However, the first bloomer suits worn by women – "bloomers" – were loose-legged, full-length trousers that gathered in at the ankles. Amelia Jenks Bloomer (1818–1894) was a public figure, as she was the publisher of the first US newspaper aimed specifically at women (*The Lily*). Since she was famous, the clothes that Amelia wore to support the new dress reform movement started to be called "Bloomer" suits and the name stuck.

Dress reform for women

Nowadays, women choose to wear items that are as comfortable or uncomfortable or as practical or impractical as they want. For men and women, there will be clothing that is appropriate for different circumstances, such as work, leisure, and sporting activities. But this has only been the case for less than 100 years. Clothing caused women many problems in the 19th century when the fight for women's rights, particularly the right to vote, known as **suffrage**, was gaining support.

Some of the styles and fabrics women were expected to wear could make simple tasks like sitting, walking, and going up and down stairs difficult or even dangerous. In the 1840s in the United States, a movement for dress reform for women started. Many of the women already working for other rights for women supported it, including Elizabeth Cady Stanton, Susan B. Anthony, and Lucretia Mott, as well as Amelia Bloomer.

This shows Amelia Bloomer in 1855 wearing a complete outfit of the type she and other women's dress reformers championed. The trousers were in a style similar to those worn by Turkish women at the time, while the overskirt or overdress worn on top kept the tops of the legs modestly covered.

By the early 1880s, a similar organization had begun in Britain. Its name was the Rational Dress Society. Its founder, Florence, Viscountess Harberton, also worked hand-in-hand with those involved in other women's causes, such as with the suffragettes and women cyclists' associations. The possessions that these women wore could say a lot about their political beliefs. Indeed, throughout the centuries people have worn clothes for various political or cultural reasons.

Not just pretty, but pretty heavy!   *i*

In the late 1840s, just before the dress reform movement, the undergarments, including petticoats, worn by a woman weighed as much as 6.35 kilograms (14 pounds). By the 1880s, there had been some improvement with the weight down to about 3.18 kilograms (7 pounds). This heavy clothing would obviously have an effect on what you could do, day to day! Things have changed a lot since then, and most women now wear underclothes that weigh no more than about 100 grams (3½ ounces).

Clothing and equality

It is no surprise that the women who were interested in women's advancement were also behind dress reform. Many middle- and upper-class women felt they had to wear tight, fashionable clothes that sometimes even deformed them. This kept women from participating equally in society and community affairs. Items like heavy petticoats and **corsets** were not just uncomfortable – they made the wearer tired, prevented them from breathing properly, and could even cause women to faint. One-armed sofas, called fainting couches, became a feature of many homes.

Cycling, war, and the vote

The cause got a boost from the popularity of bicycling in the late 19th century. A new version of bloomers made for cycling, a puffy split skirt that ended halfway between knee and ankle, became popular. During World War I, women doing factory work had to dress appropriately for the job.

By the end of the 1920s, many women could vote (see page 59). Women's clothes became more unstructured, there were special outfits for sport and leisure, and their heavy petticoats soon disappeared. To find out more, try researching some of these individuals and topics: suffragettes, Married Women's Property Act, the 1848 Seneca Falls Declaration, and Emmeline or Christabel Pankhurst.

Zoom in: Who was "Purple" Perkin?

If your favourite colour was purple, before the 1860s you would not have been able to express your preference through the possessions you wore. The only purple dye available then was made from a very rare, expensive type of snail shell. For this reason, purple was identified with royalty, as important rich people were the only ones who could afford it. Then, in 1856, an 18-year-old British chemistry student, William Henry Perkin, discovered a chemical formula he could use to create a **synthetic** purple dye. Suddenly, purple clothes were affordable and became ridiculously popular. William Perkin became known as "Purple" Perkin. To find out more about this and other colour fashions through history, look online or in encyclopaedias. Try searching for William Perkin, synthetic dyes, or the Perkin medal.

Make a connection: Clothes – the possessions that reflect society's changes

Changes in the styles of the possessions we wear, such as our clothes, shoes, and jewellery, often mirror changes in society. The clothes of the 1960s and 1970s were quite different from those of the previous 50 years. The picture below shows the kind of clothes that young people wore in the 1960s.

Why do you think clothes looked like this? The growth of youth "pop" culture, and an increase in those in higher education, helped make the fashions worn by teenagers and young adults, like loon trousers and the mini skirt, popular.

By the 1980s, professional businesswomen started wearing skirt suits styled more like those worn by men. There were large shoulder pads in the jackets, which made the women look broader across the shoulders. These outfits were given the nickname "power suits" to show that women intended to "dress for success" and workplace equality with men. Ask relatives in your family who were teenagers or young adults between 1960 and 1990 for photographs of what their clothes looked like, and what people around them dressed like. Research the clothing and try to guess when the photos were taken.

Research roadshow:
Mum's wedge sandals – and more!

When Alice wanted to dress as a hippie for a fancy dress party, she thought she might have to search charity shops, or pay high prices for **retro** or vintage items. She got a dress from a friend, but still needed shoes. The answer to the problem was close at hand: she found a pair of hippie-style sandals decorated with embroidered flowers stored in the loft at home. Alice's mum had saved up to buy them in the early 1970s, but when the shoes dropped out of fashion some time afterwards, she couldn't bear to get rid of them.

Alice didn't have to leave her house to find the perfect hippie shoes. Ask if you have any old clothes in your house. Try to work out the ages of these family garments using online sources, books, and old magazines.

What other clothing possessions were there in the loft that could tell the story of her family? Some things were interesting and beautiful, such as a dress worn by her mum to a school ball and her parents' wedding outfits. Then there were the embarrassing things, like her dad's lilac nylon shirt.

One surprising thing was a very old-fashioned set of completely black clothes. After talking to older family members, Alice discovered that the black outfit was over 100 years old! It was a mourning suit that had belonged to her great-great-great-aunt. A mourning suit was a set of clothes worn by a woman for a period of time after her husband or another close relative died.

The suit in the loft consisted of a long skirt, high-necked blouse, jacket, hat, and several undergarments. There was even a white hankie with a black edge embroidered around it. By researching the style on the internet, Alice identified the suit as being from the late 19th century or early 20th century.

The most amazing **find** was a full ceremonial Japanese child's kimono, including a hat and special slippers. How did that end up in her family's loft? It turned out that almost 20 years earlier, her family had been hosts for a Japanese exchange teacher. The teacher, Yashimi, had presented them with the kimono as a thank-you gift. The story behind each of these items added to Alice's understanding of the history of the family. She was pleased that her parents had kept them.

What can you find?

See if any clothes still in your house or the homes of older relatives are representative of specific times over the last few generations. Old school uniforms or college scarves might give you information about the schools or universities your family attended. To keep this information from being lost, consider photographing interesting garments and creating a provenance record with all you find out.

A WOODLAND SPEAR POINT: DIGGING UP THE PAST

Some people's prized possessions are not carefully passed down through families, or they are sold to buy other things. Some quite interesting and valuable items can end up under our feet in the ground. They need to be dug up to find out about them and their owners. This is how archaeologists found spear points thousands of years old at Garvies Point on Long Island near the edge of New York City.

Left behind for us to find

Are you criticized by family or friends for not being careful enough with your possessions? If so, you could give them a good excuse: if no one in the past dropped, threw away, hid, or lost their possessions, there would be no finds for archaeologists to discover!

Many of the objects found by archaeologists are like pieces in a puzzle that can gradually reveal what life was like at specific times in the past. These possessions from the past are particularly important when it is **prehistoric** people being studied. This is because they did not use a written language to record their history. The objects have to tell the story for them.

Garvies Point and the past

What would your possessions say to someone who didn't know you? Would they tell an observer 2,000 years from now how old you were, what your sex is, if you are rich or poor, or educated? With no written records, would the observer even know what many of your possessions are or what they are used for? These are the problems faced by the archaeologists and historians dealing with prehistoric sites.

This is true of stone spear points and other stone objects, like those found at Garvies Point (visit their website to find out more about the place: **www. garviespointmuseum.com**). For example, it is impossible to know just by looking at spear points what they were used for. They could have been used for hunting, for protection from wild animals, or to defend one group from another group of prehistoric humans.

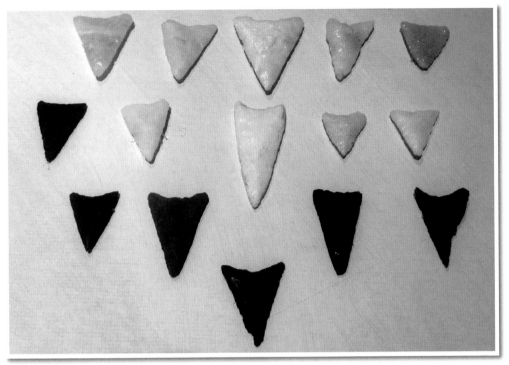

The areas around Garvies Point Museum in Long Island are some of the most vibrant and populated in the world today. But during the time when these stone spear points were being used, it was a case of day-to-day survival in a hostile environment.

Today we think of Stone Age people as primitive, but their tools and objects were difficult to make and took great skill and patience. The range of the objects they had for different purposes is astonishing.

Stone tools, usually made from flint and chert, were very good at doing the jobs they were made for. See if you can find any experimental archaeology videos on YouTube and watch how flint is knapped (carved by breaking off small pieces) and how prehistoric tools can be used to cut down trees or attached to wood to make spears or arrows.

It might also be worth using a search engine on the Internet to see the lumps of flint and chert which were eventually pared down to the tools you can see in the picture above. You can then appreciate the time it took to form these tools!

Context

Archaeologists need to know if objects are in their original context when they find possessions belonging to people of the past. This means, are they in the place, or near the place, where they were left all those years ago? Asking these questions is important, because it is the only way to work out what objects go together. For example, when archaeologists digging up stone tools and weapons then uncover a modern roll of barbed wire in the soil underneath the stone finds, they know the context has been disturbed. How can this happen? Weather conditions, such as floods and erosion, can cause things from various places and different time periods to be mixed up. Human activity, such as agriculture and stone quarrying, can also move things like topsoil and gravel from one place to somewhere else many kilometres away.

Prehistoric periods

Palaeolithic Early Stone Age with human-like hunters and gatherers

Mesolithic Middle Stone Age, only in Europe, with modern human hunters and gatherers

Neolithic New Stone Age with agriculture developing

Bronze Age Humans start making things from bronze

Iron Age Humans start making things from iron

> *i*
>
> The term "lithic" as used in the words "palaeolithic", "mesolithic", and "neolothic", means something to do with, or using, stone. It comes from the ancient Greek word *lithikos* which means stone.

Although the term "stone age" just stands for the time before ancient peoples had the technology to make things out of metal, this can be a different period of time in different places. These palaeolithic hand axes were made during the stone age of the south-west desert area in what is now Libya, in Africa. Even some of the remotest people in the world tend to use some metal now.

Where should I look?

Museums and historical reconstructions are the best places to find out about the lives of prehistoric peoples, because our understanding of their lives is based only on the physical objects they left behind. It is helpful to see the possessions themselves and how they might have been used. Most large historical museums have prehistoric objects found in their region and representative objects from other sites around the world. You can also get your hands dirty! Ask at local museums or historical societies if there are any archaeological digs you could volunteer to help on. The Young Archaeologists' Club can point you in the right direction (**www.yac-uk.org**). There are branch clubs with activities, training days, and field walking trips.

Metal detectors and treasure troves

Stone Age sites like Garvies Point don't contain metal objects from the prehistoric past. When archaeologists are digging through areas that do have metal objects, it is possible to use metal detectors to search for finds. These objects can range from coins to swords to belt buckles to jewellery.

Sometimes it can be much more. When large numbers of objects, such as coins, are all found together, it usually means that a **hoard** was purposefully hidden or buried. These places need proper archaeological exploration and the finds need protecting. In most countries, there are laws that cover situations like this. In the United Kingdom, the Treasure Act of 1996 lays down regulations for deciding the ownership and value of treasure hoards. Each county also has a person who deals with special finds under a programme called the Portable Antiquities Scheme.

Mystery objects

i

Archaeologists are often mystified by many of the objects they discover. Sometimes, these things are objects whose purposes have not yet been fully understood. Occasionally, archaeologists say that these prehistoric possessions were probably used in some kind of **ritual**, or a spiritual or religious ceremony. This might be true, but it is also the case that these things could be parts of toys, games, or even practical items used in ways that we don't yet know about. Who knows what someone in 2,000 years will make of pieces of Lego or small action figure toys that we leave behind, and how they will imagine these possessions were used.

For example, in 2013 a mystery object was examined at a museum open day in the US state of Montana. It was a prehistoric animal rib bone decorated with carved incisions in the form of slashes and X marks. The expert thought it might be a tally stick for recording the number of something, but he really wasn't sure. Could it be a ritual item, a message, a toy, or even a love token?

This recreated Woodlands Native American village shows you the kind of environment these people lived in. Not many possessions have survived from these complex societies, compared with the large numbers of **artefacts** found in warm and dry places, like the Middle East. This is because of soil and weather conditions, as well as the materials many of the buildings and objects were made of.

All kinds of metal objects can be found. This is a picture of an Iron Age object, the Gundestrup Cauldron. It is made of silver and it was found in a peat bog in Denmark. It is now in a museum in the country's capital, Copenhagen.

YOUR POSSESSIONS, YOUR LIFE

In time, some of your possessions might become heirlooms to your **descendants**. It is worth thinking about the objects around you, and how to protect and preserve those that already have a long history, as well as possessions you want to survive into the future.

Ask the right questions in time

People often see things such as a clock or a picture on the wall and think it's old or "boring". Then, by the time they are interested, it's too late. Anyone who could explain the object's history is gone or has forgotten.

You can keep this from happening in your house if you identify things that seem interesting or old and ask about them. Keep notes and make computer records of what you find out, or make provenance records like the one shown on page 11. Other people will read your notes, so you need to be clear. Writing, "This beautiful mirror belonged to Grandma. She got it when she was six from Aunt Mags...", does not provide enough information. You create a much more useful piece of evidence if you write, "This mirror belonged to Ann Elizabeth Kendall Nelson. She got it on her sixth birthday, 12 November 1947, from Margaret Kendall, her father's sister."

Keeping things safe

From Beanie Babies to diamond tiaras, your possessions will survive better if they are stored in the right way. If you think about the different categories of items you want to preserve, you can research the best options. Find out about special products, such as acid-free garment boxes to store old clothing. Check that photographs are not bent or placed where they stick together. You can get advice from the internet, from antique shops, and archive material suppliers.

However, if you are unlucky or careless, your possessions can be lost or stolen. It is possible to use special invisible marking pens for some items, particularly things made of wood, metal, or plastic. Small things, such as jewellery, should be photographed and possibly insured. Some police forces give advice on how to protect your possessions or run schemes to permanently mark possessions like bicycles.

Family possessions are often tucked away in boxes or drawers until no one knows what they are or whom they belonged to. Don't let this happen to your family! If you make yourself the family historian and archivist, you can find out about the possessions before it is too late.

Personal and family possessions for the future

Think about holding on to some personal and family keepsakes for the future. Maybe you have judo belts or swimming badges that you worked hard for. Perhaps you want to preserve memories by keeping the first CD you ever bought, for example, even if you don't like the music any more. These possessions are a part of your history.

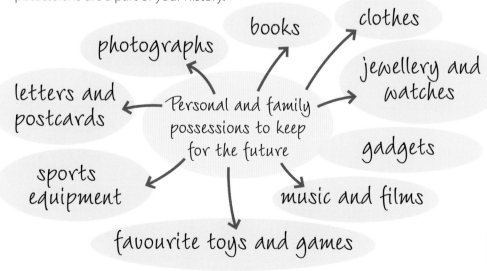

books

clothes

photographs

jewellery and watches

letters and postcards

Personal and family possessions to keep for the future

gadgets

sports equipment

music and films

favourite toys and games

TIMELINE

This timeline sets out some of the world's most famous and important inventions in chronological order. There are brief descriptions of those you may not be familiar with. Places heavily featured in the main text are marked in **bold**.

1840 First postage stamps in the UK

1844 First telegraph message sent

1847 First country-wide postage stamps in the United States

1856 Method of mass-producing steel developed by Henry Bessemer

1858 Sewing machine patented by Elias Howe

1873 Jeans first made in San Francisco by Levi Strauss

1876 **Telephone invented by Alexander Graham Bell**

1877 Phonograph (record player) invented by Thomas Edison

1887 First modern cars created by Karl Benz

1896 Wireless (radio) patented by Guglielmo Marconi

1902 **First teddy bears produced**

1903 Crayons invented by Binney and Smith

1907 First synthetic plastic, Bakelite, invented by Leo Baekeland

1908 **First Model T Ford produced**

1926 Television first demonstrated by John Logie Baird

1931 Beginning of stereo sound recording

1932 Technicolor film process is perfected

1935 Monopoly game concept sold to the Parker Brothers; first tape recorder invented by Joseph Begum; Nylon invented by DuPont labs

1940 Modern colour television invented by Peter Goldmark

1943 Ballpoint pen patented by László Bíró

1944 First automatic digital computer designed by H. Aiken

1947 **Technology needed for wireless mobile phones developed**

1948 Transistors devised by US team of Bardeen, Brattain, and Shockley

1953 Transistor radio by Texas Instruments goes on sale

1956 First computer hard disk; video tape recorder developed by Charles Ginsberg

1958 Computer modem invented

1959 Barbie dolls first appeared; microchip invented by both Jack Kilby and Robert Noyce

1962 Audio cassette invented; *Spacewar!* video game developed

1970 Compact disc (CD) technology patented by James Russell

1971 Video cassette and VCR invented

1972 Word processor developed

1981 First personal computer, the IBM-PC, invented

1985 Windows program devised by Microsoft

1990 World Wide Web, Internet Protocol (HTTP), and WWW language (HTML) created by Sir Tim Berners-Lee

1995 DVD invented

2001 First personal MP3 player, the iPod, developed by Apple

2007 First smartphone, the Apple iPhone, introduced

APPENDIX

Women's suffrage

Women were given the vote in different countries at different times. This table shows some of the dates.

Country	Year
Australia	1902
China	1949
France	1944
India	1950
New Zealand	1893
South Africa	1930 (white women), 1994 (black women)
Switzerland	1971
United Kingdom	1918 (married women over 30), 1928 (all women 21 and over)
United States	1920

GLOSSARY

antique something dating from a period long ago. Some people think a true antique must be at least 100 years old.

artefact object or tool belonging to an earlier culture, stage, or time period

assembly line factory method in which parts are added in a particular order to create a finished product

bequest money or possession given to someone in a will

cellular-digital in wireless personal phones, a system that can transmit data digitally

census official counting of the population, and collection of other statistics

component one part of an item made up of many different parts

consumer society society where the economy is based on the buying and selling of products to consumers

context conditions or events that can affect something's meaning

corset very tight fitting undergarment worn on the torso

curio small, interesting object

descendant person descended from an ancestor. You are your parents' descendant.

dispatches official messages sent by an officer from a war zone

disposable income amount of money someone has left to spend after paying for essentials, such as housing, bills, and food

document in history, a written piece of evidence

domestic relating to the home or household

enlisted military personnel who are not officers

evaluate work out if something is important or true

evidence in history, anything that helps create an accurate picture of the past

find in archaeology, the objects found in the ground

genealogy study of family ancestries and histories

heritage past or things from the past

hoard large group of artefacts, such as coins

inherit receive something from an older generation

Latin language of the Romans

limited edition when only a specific number of something is produced

logbook official, written record kept by those in the military or in education

maritime related to the navy or the sea

mass-produced making standard items in large numbers

materialism when there is a big interest in money and possessions

memorabilia things kept as reminders of memorable events or possessions

memorial something designed as a way of remembering the dead

movement in clocks and watches, the mechanical parts that make them work

munitions all the materials, such as weapons and ammunition, used to fight a war

oral history historical evidence recorded on tape or written down as spoken

patent rights given to a person who invents or designs something

porcelain high-quality ceramic material

prehistory time in the history of a place before there were any written records

primary source historical source that dates from the period itself

provenance origin and history of something

reliable likely to be true or accurate

retro imitating a style or design from the past

ritual practice carried out for religious or spiritual reasons

secondary source historical source produced after the event

space race technological competition in the 1960s and 1970s between the USA and the USSR to be the most successful at space travel and exploration

suffrage right to vote

synthetic human-made material

trade directory published list with addresses of shops and different professionals in the 19th century before there were telephone books

trade route route used to take goods from one country or area to another

unethical not following the rules and standards of right conduct

vintage old item that is a good example of a style or design from the past

will document containing instructions for what to do with a person's belongings after he or she dies

FIND OUT MORE

Books

A History of the World in 100 Objects, Neil MacGregor (Penguin, 2012)

The Changing Role of Women Since 1900 (Research It!), Louise Spilsbury (Heinemann Library, 2010)

Twentieth Century (Collins History), Alf Wilkinson *et al.* (Collins, 2010)

World War I (Research It!), Stewart Ross (Heinemann Library, 2010)

World War II (Research It!), Andrew Langley (Heinemann Library, 2010)

Magazines

BBC History Magazine
This highly illustrated magazine is full of interesting articles about people, objects, and events.

Hindsight Magazine
This magazine is aimed mainly at GCSE history students, but it has many interesting articles written by historians about the 20th century. The articles include primary sources and other documentary evidence.

Websites

www.bbc.co.uk/bitesize/ks3/history
This website covers many important periods in history, including the Tudors and Stuarts, the industrial era, and the 20th century.

www.nationalarchives.gov.uk/education/topics/topics-ks3.htm
The National Archives website can be used to find many topics you may be interested in or happen to be studying. It includes scans of original documents and other primary sources that you can use to support your research.

Places to visit

The best way to see interesting objects that belonged to people in the past is to go to a museum. At historical reconstruction sites, you can see how people in the past used their possessions.

Blist Hill Victorian Town Museum
www.ironbridge.org.uk

The British Museum
www.britishmuseum.org

Butser Ancient Farm Iron Age Village
www.butserancientfarm.co.uk

The Museum of Childhood
www.edinburghmuseums.org.uk/Venues/Museum-of-Childhood

The Victoria and Albert Museum
www.vam ac.uk

Further research

Learn more about your possessions and other interesting objects by doing further research on these things, topics, events, and individuals:

- Try to find out about the most valuable baseball cap.

- Find out about a famous toy or game, such as Etch-a-Sketch or Monopoly, and how it was made and the people behind it.

- Research the Victoria Cross (VC) medal and how it is made.

- Get out a family photograph and try to date it using the clothing worn and the method of photography used.

- Investigate the history of listening to music, from the phonograph to the cassette player to the CD player to MP3 players.

- Find out about some of the special stamp designs of the last 20 years and whom they commemorated.

- The bicycle became an important possession for many people over 100 years ago. Starting with your bike, find out as much as you can about the bicycle and its place in the history of transport and leisure.

- Make a full timeline from the 1940s of the skateboard and its development, including important figures such as Frank Nasworthy and Alan Gelfand.

- Look into the history of a piece of clothing you own.

INDEX